Also by Mary Bradish O'Connor

Calabash
with Johanna M. Bedford, Jane Harris Austin
and M.L. Harrison Mackie

Say Yes Quickly

A CANCER TAPESTRY

MARY BRADISH O'CONNOR

POT SHARD PRESS

1997

Thanks to the following magazines in which some of these poems
first appeared:
> Lynx: A Journal for Linking Poets
> Tanka Splendor 1996
> Hummingbird: Magazine of the Short Poem

The title and epigram are taken from *Open Secret: Versions of Rumi*,
translations by John Moyne and Coleman Barks, originally published by
Threshold Books, 139 Main Street, Brattleboro, VT 05301.

Reference in Rumination 4 is to Rachel Naomi Remen, *Kitchen Table
Wisdom: Stories that Heal*, Riverhead Books, 1996, page 93.

Thanks to Alchemy for the image in the last line of "Dear Friends."

Book and cover design by Elizabeth Petersen
Cover tapestry, "Puye Vista, 1991," by Ellen Athens
Published by Pot Shard Press, Post Office Box 215, Comptche, CA 95427
First printing, October 1997
Manufactured in the United States of America

Publisher's Cataloging-in-Publication
(Provided by Quality Books, Inc.)

O'Connor, Mary Bradish.
    Say yes quickly : a cancer tapestry / Mary Bradish O'Connor.
  p. cm.
  ISBN: 0-9656052-1-3

    1. Cancer—Poetry. I. Title.
PS3565.C67S39 1997   811'.54
                        QBI97-30291

Is what I say true? Say yes quickly,
if you know, if you've always known it
from the beginning of the universe.

— Rumi

CONTENTS

For Marty
who never forgot
she married a poet

INTRODUCTION

This early morning I am remembering stories I have heard and seen of mothers passing their memories to their daughters and grandmothers spinning the past for their grandchildren. As I am remembering these things, I feel once again the discord, the broken cord, the lost chord inside me because for me there is no one to tell. My lost womb was always empty. So into whose well of remembrance do I pour my stories while my heart still beats?

The Luba people create memory boards with beads or with impressions carved inside them so that they can pass memories from one generation to the next. The memory teller passes her hand over the beads and according to the arrangement—linear, circular, many beads, one large bead—she tells the story. The story depends upon the audience, the current politics, the weather, whatever is in the air. The beads and impressions remind the teller but do not directly *tell* the teller what to say. In this way, memory can be told according to what it is: a river that flows and ripples and moves and reveals, jostled by what contains it and what it encounters on its journey.

Our bodies, too, are repositories of memory. The scars on my hands remind me of stories from my childhood. The unsoftened shape of my head reminds me of cancer stories and the chemo-therapy infusion center. All my life I have looked down upon these strong tanned forearms, living memory boards to be read.

But to whom? There is no more time to mourn my unborn daughter. Cancer prompts me to create my own memory board now, as the wind is rising. Yes or no? I say yes quickly and conjure this: amber beads on a redwood slab, impressions carved into the heartwood, shard of memory left in the clearing for a stranger to find.

Yes, I say, and fling myself into the hot springs of experience, and begin to write.

Ready or Not

REVERIE/REVISION

A summer evening.
Neighbors talk quietly
from their front stoops
across the yards and street.
On the ambient twilight breeze
float hints of dinner's hamburger
and onions, shrill children's voices
counting backward, shouting
ally-ally-in-free.
Soon the children will bathe,
dress in fresh cotton pajamas
and enfolded by their mothers
lie down on tight white sheets.

They will rest
in the complacent swollen silence
of a world made safe for democracy
while tanker trucks
rumble down narrow streets
their hoses putt-putt-putting
surging clouds of sweet-smelling
DDT, laying its mantle
across the innocents.

A BODY IS THE REPOSITORY OF MEMORY

These Hands

are the hands of my mother
smoothly peeling potatoes
with a worn paring knife,
spirals unfolding around
small white buds about
to become pancakes.
This scar is when I almost drowned
going out to the deep end,
flinging up my arms at the last minute
into the iron fence,
round hole on a thin white wrist.
Grandma cautioned, "stop
cracking your knuckles
or your fingers will be crooked"
and they are.
These hands fingered guitar chords
in the dorm room,
wore a tiny gold and green engagement
ring proudly and with great
relief then nothing for a while
now another gold band
this one for good.
I remember my mother next to me
at the kitchen table, taking
my hands,
pushing back the cuticle on each
finger, filing the nails
with a soft emery board,
and then oh
joy
she polished each nail in red

enamel. "Here," she said,
"here's how you'll do this
when you grow up,"
and she smiled
and I smiled, my hands
warm and safe inside
her hands.

These Eyes

rest upon the salt-fired vase.
Afternoon sun slants across it
high to low
and I remember the night
and the fire
that transformed it.
I am ambushed by
the angle of light
the tangle of blue daisies.
Who else will see
the substance of this little vase
a lump of clay
a bag of salt
imprints of Steve's hands
ash and salt and radiance
set on the polished surface
of a poet's desk?
Light shifts and lowers.
Smoky glimmers darken
and melt into ordinary.
Still, I linger longer
holding it
with these eyes.

These Arms

spread wide on each side
as I float face up
in the canyon hot springs.
Lapis sky surrounds
looming salmon bluffs.
Hawks ride the canyon thermals.
Sandwiched between sun
and sulfur,
floating in amniotic
waters,
my own heart's beat
measures time.
I embrace the universe
with these arms.

THE PRESENCE OF THE ABSENCE

At the cafe we were three,
then two and me.
Talking about tough years mothering,
grandmothering,
raising daughters and sons,
they sailed onward. I was silent,
near tears.
One more time I wished
I belonged to the club.
Don't. Won't.
Waited for the wind to change,
to blow them back to me.
It did.

THE HEARTLAND OF AMERICA

I

Abie drove a wagon
through neighborhood streets
he had a beard and wild
black curly hair
under his cap
his horse walked slowly
head down
he smelled bad
he collected rags
he was the only Jew I knew.

II

White every place I looked
every porch stoop and store
every street corner
black faces only passing through
at the train station
calling all aboarrrrd
to someplace else
someplace free.

III

How far can a poet move
toward tolerance and openness
with a white face
and a hometown where
fifteen or twenty Daughters
of the American Revolution
gathered after the Memorial Day parade
and sang Tenting Tonight
sprinkling rose petals

over the well-tended grave
of the hometown boy
Joseph McCarthy
such a sainted man
hounded to an early grave
by those communists
and atheists.

IV

This is your home too,
your heart's land.

V

Where I am: here
by the sea in a sea
of white. Words
flow easily, rose petals
on Dr. King's grave
but what about East Oakland?
I see myself in a Midwest mirror
as I look away from the bulldyke
as I cross the street from the young black man
as I judge my hometown neighbors
as I say *they're so ignorantracistsexist*
but never
I am like them
even now here
those words don't come
might not be true
might be true.
I dream another world:
namaste
hands together we bow
gravely and with full attention
we salute each other
honoring the god within.

GHOSTS

Another year, another Halloween
come round, rain, and a lopsided moon.
Goblin children's upturned faces gleam
like hungry birds, then turn too soon
to the neighbor's house. Sanderlings at dusk
on a glimmering street, the children scatter
into parents' arms, as little ones must,
and lights go out in living rooms later.
Innocents nestle in their goodnights,
content with treasures of chocolate bars
next to their beds. Dreams drift in amber lights
and the lonely shshshsh of passing cars.
Halloween is the night when spirits roam,
bittersweet, all their children going home.

TAROT READING BEFORE CANCER

Stand on your head.
Turn your world upside down.
Put your head where your feet are
and listen. There is a snake waiting.
The edifice you have been
will burst into flames and topple.
The dragon will place his mouth on yours
and blow.
You will feel the heat of new life,
the cold of toppled stones.
You will feel the eye of God upon you
as your protection crumbles
and fire moves through.
Then there will be gold in abundance.
This new world,
this new you in the old world,
will be all that you need it to be.

READY OR NOT

All this time trying to empty out
my belly
to move things through
and now
I see I am filled
with tears.
A lump of grief
sits like a stone
waiting.
I place my hands around my belly
tenderly holding all I have carried
through this long working year,
storms and an old dog lost,
a good friend almost gone.
Feeling knots and lumps
the nests of pain
mysterious bulges and gurgles,
I am surprised, baptized in salty waters.
I embrace myself in silence
while rumblings begin
within.

IN THE CARDS

On Mother's Day they said
You must raise your arm,
hold the sword firmly
and fight the black swirling clouds
that obscure vision.
If you do this, you will ride
the chariot of fire.
The lion will lead you everywhere;
you only need to hold the reins loosely.
You will burst into flames and fly.
In time, emerging
from the volcano, you will stand
transformed, complete.
Pregnant with male and female,
holding a crystal wand,
you will contain all the earth
even as you stand on it.
Then, finally,
you will give birth.

Now I see
I was carrying cancer even then.
Perhaps it was that day
a single cell attached
itself to my liver
and went to work.
Is this what was promised?
Have I burst into flames?
Am I in the belly of the volcano
or is it in me?
How can I give birth
without my
ovaries?

turning my face
into winter's gale—
quick!
take my temperature
is this illness or life?

*Seated at the head of a long battered conference table in the doctors'
lounge of the local hospital, primary physician on my right hand and
oncologist on my left. Rising numbers. What the tumor board said.
Which chemotherapies could be worth trying. Old coffee in paper cups.
The moment when I saw that no one really knew what to do next. My
questions. Their quiet answers.*

*An hour later I walked to the parking lot considering these things:
my tumor was growing; she thought I would live for two years after the
tumor came back; I would probably die from a failure to thrive, without
very much pain. I drove to the ocean also knowing these things: I want
to hold on to sweet life; there is no more time for idle speculation about
where God is; this part of the cycle is a mystery to everyone.*

*Tears and large long swells of ocean waves. The surprise and shock
of meeting my mortality, seeing a probable path laid out before me—
mine, my dying journey. The comfort of a big ocean and a small me.
The brilliance of yellow flowers on ice plants for miles, as far as I could
see. The wind blew across my curls. Not very much pain. Counted the
months of two years after recurrence from that very moment, bargain-
ing, stretching time. Cried all the way home, driving through a rainy,
blustery afternoon.*

*And now the morning after, DAY ONE after, just another morning
with a run to the post office. In the midst of the trip to town, a small
desperate voice says "drive fast, drive away," and another voice calmly
answers "just enjoy the drive."*

THE NEWS

Stale food and coffee smells
in the doctors' lounge
a doctor on each side
telling the news
about the numbers
separating hope
from possibility.
In this ordinary moment
another part of my journey begins.

And so
I step out
into yellow flowers
along the haul road above the ocean.
Sea wind blows around my downy head.
The ocean sweeps and circles the shoreline,
disappearing into the lost coast.
Standing on this peaceful rim
among wild irises
sea figs
beach strawberries
I am cushioned by life.
I know I am not alone
and I understand
I am.

STORMY WEATHER

This varnished morning
the horizon holds new spaces
where yesterday's bull pines
and cypresses stood.
Blown over in one night's storm,
they rest on muddy ground,
trunks broken open like ripe
mangoes, tangled arms angled
up and sideways.
After everlasting night,
we are numb in the wind's wake.
All power is out on the coast.
In time, we will train our eyes
to hold a new horizon
but this anguished morning
we begin to live in a damaged world
where we must use the light well.
We hunker down in our fragile
lives and reluctantly
turn to catastrophe.

FOR MARTY

Vague memories after surgery
of a deep rich voice alongside
saying "wake up. Come on, wake up"
and being dropped onto a narrow bed,
alien grunts of Ugh! Ugh! Ugh!
from deep inside.

Rain ran down the window.
A bell rang when I pushed the button
because my belly hurt.
Warm hands smoothed my forehead
while familiar voices hushed me
back to sleep.

Waking to see a patch of light
in the open doorway and you
sitting there on the floor
looking out, looking back at me
in the silence of a half-dark
hospital room.

Like an amulet carried close
to my heart, the memory of that long
pain-racked night, you sitting
in a pool of light, leaning
against the door, keeping
quiet faith, keeping
watch while I swam
fathoms away.

THE CURE PILE

antioxidants   coffee enemas   carrot juice
colon irrigation   meditation   radiation
stress reduction   green tea
the bark of the yew tree   prayer
macrobiotics   aerobics   fasting
tea made from roots   wild yams
crystals blessed by the Dalai Lama   pets
ginger   Siberian ginseng   garlic
calf's liver juice   tamoxifen
acupuncture   cutting the tumor out
psychic healing   being celibate
mistletoe   ashes   heat
support groups   yoga   zinc tablets

who I am

is a woman
whose ovaries
are cancerous.
I am
the same person I was
yesterday
only yesterday
I didn't know
who I am.

The wind gusts and the tall skinny redwoods click together like sticks while I lie on my back, shade my eyes with my hand and look at the blue uncluttered sky. Tops of the few remaining bull pines wave in and out of view. I close my eyes and think: all my life I have lain in the sun, soaking sunlight deep inside.

I never thought I would die of cancer. How could I leave this planet, trees sparkling against an unblemished sky, cat stretched out next to me under the shaded bench. Reflection in the patio door: round head with blond stubble, veins pulsing along temples, ribs, sunken belly containing mystery, sturdy brown legs. Who is this person? Me. Whose is this body? Mine. I could leave here. I could die. I turn over in the sunshine. I feel the sun on my shoulders. I fall asleep in the sound of the windchimes.

THE INFUSION CENTER

We are a tribe of turbaned women.
We decorate our heads as best we can
with rhinestones
jaunty caps
plain black wraps
multicolored scarves.
We sit quietly while chemicals flow
through our veins.
We doze, we read,
we make desultory conversation.
We watch each other and smile
as we shuffle to the bathroom.
Each of us has a secret under our hat:
we are gutsy and angry and fierce
in our desire to live.
We intend to survive even this toxic
indignity. I wonder
why we don't rise up as one woman
take off our turbans
reveal the tender curves
of our brave heads
and say to all who so smoothly quote
numbers and charts and statistics:
"Hey! Take a look.
This is cancer.
This is courage.
This is me."

CHEMO MEMO

waiting for life
to return to these old bones
a trip to the city
a long week ago today:
chemotherapy

sitting here alone
awake at 2 a.m.
I thought there were two
on this chemo journey
who was I kidding

why be furious
donkey does the best she can
carrying loads
of taxol and cisplatin
longing to kick up her heels

overwhelmed body
has reached its limit
polluted estuary
can't filter, can't cleanse
too many toxic chemicals

spring jonquils bloom
in the meadow where no one
has walked for years
I decided today
to live for a while

SUNDAY NAP

The woodstove is quirky, has been all day,
reluctant to burn even our dry oak.
Red embers turn black and cold and I lay
the fire again, hoping it will burn. Smoke

fills the chamber, kindling catches, becomes
ashes, then nothing. No spark, no bright flame,
no warmth. Weary and woolly headed, dumb
as the iron stove itself, I blame

the chemotherapy, the weather, all
manner of things, but still there is no spark.
Between me and passionate fire, a wall
of inertia and fog and fear of the dark.

Give it up. Beat a strategic retreat.
Tomorrow perhaps there'll be light and heat.

LAST LIGHT

When winter storms come
and life shrinks to a kerosene circle,
it is all waiting and watching,
blown out of our hands,
an island of light in a dark world.
We try to read. We try to sleep.

Power returns in its own time.
Then we walk from room to room
leisurely, thinking of other things,
dinner perhaps, or the weekend,
and the spacious world is open again.
We forget to write. We forget to pray.

Still, at night when the last light burns,
we remember the wind and how quickly it turns.

day two after chemo
twilight can't come soon enough
sick and tired of it
a woman with cancer waiting
for this precious day to end

Cancer and a rainy morning bring me to boxes of my old college notebooks and musty journals that have been shipped across the country and moved from house to house at least five times. Sitting on the floor next to the closet, I spend the morning rereading these journals and notebooks and shuffling through old photographs, remembering earlier years of righteousness and desperation and being in love and exploring the world and seeking my place in the circle.

Dog-eared photographs reveal a younger, thinner, healthier me, dear friends, old friends, used-to-be friends, dogs, cats, rabbits, horses. The same words fall out of the pages over and over: freedom, lonely, love, afraid, should, where, God. On this drizzly morning, these desperate notes to myself don't seem very important.

Time to jettison the baggage and travel lighter. Two large black plastic garbage bags filled with thin bound notebooks, half-completed journals, loose pages, photos, birthday cards and old letters (I'm getting married, I'm getting divorced, I love you, get well). Rain blows against the windows while I journey one more time through my life, preparing documents for the compost pile. Cancer forces me to carry my memories in my pocket. It's time to haul the bags away.

MIDNIGHT CANCER

is a bottomless pit
where voices echo
around and around
endlessly
repeating the same
prayer:
oh
God
why
me?
Sooner or later, midnight
cancer changes to
morning cancer,
brighter,
more hopeful.
Somewhere the sun
rises warm and round.
Birds are singing.
After a while,
morning cancer melts
into afternoon cancer
where it hides among chores:
cut the grass
clean the downspouts
drain the noodles.
Later, the house falls silent
and even the dog is asleep.
There might or might not be rain.
Without a sound
you are falling,
arms wide and circling.
It's midnight.
You have cancer.

CHEMO BRAIN

These slow empty days
life is reduced to the small
picture:
not Bosnia
but oranges in a market
rolling on the ground
alongside the woman's body
after the shell hit;
winter trees reflected in a muddy puddle;
the flash of a hawk's red breast.
On turtle time, I have no protection
from life's little knives
and no energy for the five-day forecast.
Outside the window a single daffodil bends low,
a light in the wind and rain.

THE INVISIBLE WOMAN

Time enough after chemo
to return to the world slowly
and with some fear.
Appearing in selected spots
supermarket
coffeehouse
bookstore
no one sees me.
Neighbors go by without a nod
to a thinner me, bald
under my cap and glasses.
The disturbing freedom of a moment
of choice:
identify myself into welcome back
or be still.
Do we share the same universe?
They don't see the old me.
They don't see the new me.
I am the same.
I will never be
the same.

STORM WARNING

We ride the old year out on howling winds
and heavy rain, seeking warmth and light
as best we can, reading desperate omens
in the alarums of a darkened night
and dirty weather. This new year's eve
does not bring meditative time and peace
or even celebration. We leave
those hopes behind with all the rest and bless
this moment of safety in a wild storm,
this circle of light that keeps fear at bay,
this fledgling faith that lets us mourn
our lost beliefs and trust a clearer day.
Listen. The wind is up and so am I,
waiting in darkness while the old year dies.

all winter waiting
for plump narcissus bulbs
to sprout green then white
now we set the plants outside
their perfume too much to endure

Mysteries carried me through chemotherapy. I don't remember the names of the authors or the plots but I remember they were neat puzzles with antisocial female detectives who jogged every morning and only had yogurt in their refrigerators. The bad person was very bad and by the end of the book all the clues added up to his and sometimes her punishment.

Life is not reasonable but a journey from mystery to mystery, Rachel Naomi Remen says in Kitchen Table Wisdom and she doesn't mean my chemo mysteries. Her mystery never or rarely reveals itself and is a puzzle that needs to be tolerated, even honored. It has some good guys and some bad guys but mostly we're in between somewhere, wandering as best we can through our days and nights. With luck we have time to breathe before the next mystery unfolds with or without our full attention.

I knew this, or thought I did, before I got cancer. Now I know it better. The first months after my diagnosis I struggled to untangle Gordian knots: where might I have gotten cancer? What should I have done differently? If I do X treatment, Y will happen and then Z, where I live if not happily, at least ever after.

I understand now that my life is not that kind of mystery; it is Remen's kind, messy and unclear, the kind where you do the best you can on any given day. I review the research, hear the doctors out, and go inside myself to make the decisions that feel best for me.

The mystery is linear in this way: my living will end in my dying. There is a House at the End of the Lane. As Principal Investigator, my task is to stay awake and to live along into the mystery. On good days, I navigate by this compass. Many days I just try to stay afloat. On bad days, I pull out the other kind of mystery and begin to read.

CA 125: BLOOD TEST

They draw my blood to do a test to see
if numbers rise or fall and thus to tell
if cancer lives. They plumb the depths of me
while we await the soundings in this hell.
Swimming toward morning and the telephone,
we talk in a quiet distracted way
and rarely touch, each struggling alone
on separate sorrow's paths, though aloud we say
life goes on. Whatever truth unfolds
tomorrow, whatever the numbers teach,
tonight we huddle mortal and cold
utterly changed, immortality breached.
Try to sleep. Tell yourself there's nothing to fear.
Another long night in a terrible year.

THE CONTAINER

First there was tumor and sage words they said
about treatment: surgery and chemo.
Then post operation, confined to bed
I thought only about trying to go

down the cluttered hallway and return,
exhausted, triumphant. When the time came
to leave the hospital womb, I learned
what was next—toxic chemical pain.

One day with Taxol and twenty without.
Five trips to the city where all depended
on solicitous nurses moving about
taking care of me. Then it all ended.

Now no one is watching and I feel the lack.
Now there is nothing but chill wind at my back.

VENERABLE BEDE IN CASPAR

I

The hummingbird shoots indoors
whirls around
almost at once begins to beat
her wings her whole self
against the skylight, dropping
tiny drops of fear
buzzing and whirring
frantic cheeping
as the brilliant sunshine pours
through the glass.
Long beak half open,
her emerald green body
rests briefly on the ledge
that supports the glass
and now her.
Small clear drops fall continuously
from her body to the ground
where they are lost.
Cat remains on full alert
while I extend the broom
bristles askew
as far as I can.

II

Every three weeks I went in
for a chemo fill-up.
Going where I was told
trying not to be sick
needles mapping my dropping bloodcount
I napped the intervening weeks

away. Through the windows I watched
winter blow the redwoods
back and forth back and forth.

Come on Sweetie. I won't
hurt you. Grab on
and you can ride out
back to your world.
Rest on this and your terror
will be over. Rest on this
for the trip home.
Throw yourself into this
unexpected predicament.
Turn away from the sun
and such desperate hope.

III

Instantaneous choices
of yes, no
hold on let go.
I give up.
After losing my uterus
after losing my ovaries
after losing my appendix
after losing my omentum
after losing my
immortality my
independence
how do I get out of here?

Flash! She's on it!
Then the truth of the short ride
then the instant of flight
green streak of light straight
to the apple tree straight
into blue freedom.

JUST SAY IT

There was a time when we were thick as thieves
when your life and mine ran similar ways
and we were close. Our recent talk retrieves
those days and I am chilled, for nothing stays
the same. What I want isn't who you are
and you want rest from deep and heavy things.
Our calls are forced, with voices faint and far
removed from juicy heart's true offerings.

What I want to say is this: I am done
with meager talk of weather and golf games.
Where were you when I was sick? Why even try
to span our different lives? Why even come
to the phone to pretend we're the same?
What I want to say is this: goodbye.

FAMILY VISIT

Soon I will have a week without you,
seven days in the Midwest in June
and it's not that it's something we can't do
because we can. We've lived in a cocoon

this last six months, just you and I, the dog,
the cats and hours of private time alone
together. Face to face, our dialogue
is clear and honest, better than the phone

can ever be, especially miles apart,
you at work all day. In a way it's time
to practice being separate but my heart
remains with you, though you are left behind.

You'll work and I'll see family, then return.
Just ordinary days one day we'll mourn.

the wind

quickens
each leaf,
each molecule of air.
All the trees bow down
and the falcon sails
upon her breath,
her breast.

Honking geese flying over the house woke me this morning. By the time I raced outside, they had moved on to the pond down the road, although for a while I could hear them calling.

A few days ago a brilliant woman in her late sixties parked her car at a local beach and walked out into the ocean to drown. A small woman whose hands never stopped shaking, she looked everywhere for relief, found none, and one early morning walked across the sand at low tide for the last time.

These two moments span the wonder of this life: waking to the primitive wild sound of geese flying overhead and the overwhelming pain carried in a tiny body out into the endless sea. As I write these words, a fierce joy surges up inside me. For the first time in weeks, I feel fully alive.

RETREAT

Imagine a glistening blue glacier
solid, forever in a high cool place,
frozen essence about to pour itself
over alabaster edges of space.

This is how it seems to the village below
but it is not how it is. The ice face
is melting, withdrawing cosmic moment
by moment, inch by inch, turning to lace

in the sun's unblinking stare. Moisture
invisibly rises transmuted without trace
into something we take on faith and falls
blessedly melting into luminous lake.

Unseeing, they call this a glacier's *retreat*.
Creedless, they call death life's greatest defeat.

CAT SCAN DECISION

So here's the decision I have to make:
whether to know if my tumor is back
or gone or do nothing at all. To take
a picture of where I am now will track

this beast along Western trails until I
die. We will know the name of the game
and be able to guess about time. Why
would I not do this? Because I would blame

all nature of aches and pain on cancer
if that is what we see. I would always
be looking at illness, no answer
for someone who loves spring's precious days.

What holds me is wellness could be what they find.
Then I'd be free to leave cancer behind.

KINDRED SPIRIT
(for K.M.M.)

For thirty years we've lived our diverse lives
apart, anchored by memories of moments
together. Yesterday's visit leaves
lingering warmth, the unswerving presence

of love that is rare, kindred and stalwart,
like you. For a while, the wind was fair
as we walked along the ocean, hearts
high as the tide, bruised souls in repair.

Once again it is autumn and you've gone
back to your life, as I now turn to mine,
the circle enlarged by your company long
after our goodbyes, back in standard time.

All those years ago, who would have guessed
how strong the connection, how deeply blessed?

SAILORS TAKE WARNING

If ever there were a time to retreat
from the world for a while, to bring forth
from silence within (or without) a sweet
pure song of consolation and faith,

that time is now. Unmoored by a future,
my little boat is adrift on a rising
tide. Even as emancipation dawns,
I cast about seeking anchorage.

Freed from likely specters of old age
and loneliness, expectations of days
everlasting, still I find myself
dreading dying's uncertain and messy ways.

As a sailor spies morning's vermilion skies,
these fears unbidden within me rise.

MATINS

White paper on smooth oak table, I wove
words late into the night, my light
mirroring yours in the house above.
I heard you call the dogs inside and slide

the reluctant door behind them.
Then silence. Then your light went out
and I was left alone with thoughts of home
and you. This poem is about

love. Last night, by choice, we slept apart
to work our crafts because we knew
this early morning I would start
back up the path again to find you.

Together, we weather night's poignant dream
of two separate lights, and darkness between.

LOVE BUILDS A BRIDGE
(for J.J.C.)

My brother called me every Tuesday
during long months of chemotherapy.
Each time he asked how I was doing
that day, then listened carefully
to my stumbling answer. We're thinking
of you, he would say, and we're hoping
tomorrow will be better. At first
he seemed a million miles away, a lost
connection, little brother long gone
down a Midwest road to a different home.
But over time love built a bridge. Apart,
in separate lives, we opened up our hearts.

Another sweet and sour irony:
cancer brought my brother back to me.

poor prayer flag
in wild winter garden
twisted and faded
all those prayers gone off
into the stormy sky

Most of the time when I write now, the poems come out as sonnets. The regular format of the structure comforts me—three four-line stanzas, ten beats to the line, a concluding rhyming couplet—so solid, so matter-of-fact. I keep within a traditional form to write about the universal experience of being mortal.

The sonnet's structure acts like a container for my wild, out-of-control emotions of fear, rage, and bitterness. It manages the chaos of cancer's intense feelings and helps me rise above banality when I describe them.

My job is to tell the truth and to keep the sonnet's structure from intruding. When the time is right, I'll head out again into more danger-ous, unmapped creative forms. For now, enough in my life is unknown. Let my friend the sonnet lead me safely on.

MIDNIGHT

What good are words when it's late at night
and the woodstove mute and spring wind blowing
silver chimes into chaos? No second sight
illuminates the dark, no sudden knowing

what to say or how it will all unfold.
Still the pencil moves across the empty page
blindly, hopefully. Stories must be told
wholly, with integrity, as we engage

in splendid life. Our ocean is wild
under a quarter moon and the tame cat cold,
curled under my arm like a trusting child.
Stars glitter with light a thousand years old.

The world is asleep. Of God there are small signs.
I pause, then begin: Once upon a time . . .

COMMONWEAL BOUQUET

Halfway down the narrow path to the beach
in early evening: a glimmering bunch
of roses and lilies in a patch
of glorious colors—orange, red, peach—
lying on the muddy ground. I found
them, green stems pointing west, frosted
with the morning's rain, casually tossed
away but not scattered. Entirely round
raindrops glistened against cream and brown
satin petals rimmed with early rot
reminding travelers of the riotous
blend of beauty and its deeper wound.
Celebration or lament left behind
at twilight for a stranger to find?

THE GRACE OF COMMONWEAL

The morning of the last day of retreat
I followed the path to an old cabin,
stark against windswept cypresses. Within,
an alabaster Buddha sat replete
with rosebud in his lap and stones and shells
surrounding, all upon a redwood altar.
The room was filled with tears and laughter,
earnest prayers of previous walkers, angels
and humans. I stood, grateful for these signs
reminding me to live in present
time and when I left, a multicolored pheasant
flew before me into the salty wind.
She left five fine feathers with this message:
others have made this cancer passage.

SHERPAS

Others have gone before me, leaving
small signs and teachings to help me find
my way. Even in the midst of grieving
daily empty spaces left behind,

I bless them, my big beautiful golden
dogs. Pumpkin had cancer deep in her throat
but didn't know it, so she raced along
the wild ocean, sand and salt in her coat,

joyful until the morning she died.
Honeyed Scooter, everyone's friend,
rose to greet them as they stepped inside
in spite of the pain he had at the end.

Filled with life all their days and nights,
they moved with grace into the great good light.

pennies and nickels
rolled and counted long ago
dreams
in a paper bag
saved for a rainy day

We took her to the beach the morning she died. We put milkbones in our pockets, brushed her golden coat one last time, and took her to her favorite ocean dunes at low tide. Feathered tail high, she ran familiar circles around us and barked at seagulls and ravens in spite of the black cancer in her throat. Like her puppy self ten years earlier, she dug holes in the wet sand, then ate it. I threw smooth brown sticks for her to chase and retrieve as we, wordless, walked the shining encircling shore.

Then we took her, damp and sandy, to the vet's office, laid down on the floor next to her, one on each side, stroked and murmured secret words into her silken ears, which started up in concern and then relaxed in trust. Finally we felt the spirit rise within her and in an instant leave her long blond body stretched out and heavy on the black-and-white-tiled floor. We left her fuzzy toy behind but I took the faded purple collar, still wet, still full of sand. I keep it in the trunk of my car next to my flares and flashlight and other emergency supplies.

BIRTHDAY PRAYER

Fifty-five years ago I left the womb
reluctantly, fell into a winter
of war and loss, anxiety and gloom-
filled days. Bereft, I missed the center

of my world, made do with what I had,
grew strong in a jovial, sanguine way.
Arriving here, I find a kind of sad
wonder that, in spite of cancer, today

I'm supposed to celebrate life, to blend
bitter and sweet, to forget any pain.
And so I give the gift of hope and send
myself some light, some sun in place of rain.

Cancer and birthdays teach me prayers: through tears
and frenzied fears, remember resolute stars.

WINTER OAK

Three years ago the big oak atop
your mountain fell during winter rains
and now you offer it to us, a crop
of firewood to heat the house again.

Together we climb the carved-out road
to weathered piles of clean split wood
spread out under noon sun. Together we load
the truck full to bursting. How could

we ever tell you what this means, this gray
gold, given freely, fruit of a storm
long past? Winter will come but this July day
friends are working together, laughing and warm.

Sturdy and seasoned as oak over time,
the gift of your friendship, love's steadfast flame.

THE WATCHMAN

Impregnable red rocks rise roundly
upward touching streaks of white-blue sky
softened by spring cottonwoods profoundly
velvet green across a roiling river. I
think I know this mountain. I have seen
the morning light blaze across her face,
slip gown-like down her base, and evening cream
turn twilight gold, then black without a trace
of brooding presence. And so to bed,
tucking in under stars and one last turning
for a mountain goodnight, soul-fed
in stone-red visions coolly burning.
Unblinking, the sentinel watchman looms—
I wonder, who is watching whom?

CHEMO TAROT

The tiger gnaws on the thigh
of the poor green fool
even as light surrounds him
expressionless
carrying a dull sword
lost in clouds
a long elephant ride
to the hierophant.
Timor mortis has settled in
like fury
the axeman's hood.
Storm front moving through.
Record lows tonight.
So cold so cold so cold

Say Yes Quickly

wolf moon rises round
above silver cypresses
now I remember
they said cancer but we're
still shining one year later

WINTER SOLSTICE

Sunrise on the day of longest night
unmasks tiny yellow birds in trees
flitting in flashes of saffron light
from branch to branch, exploding at the least
sound. Tawny thrushes scour the muddy ground
for breakfast and I scratch through the year's
leavings, seeking seeds to crack. Background
sounds of ravens cawing hoarsely: have no fear.
Remembering surgery and cancer,
chemo days that hung like smoke in rain,
I bring hard questions, find no answers
only golden birds, tiny votive flames.
She says, now you've finally begun
to walk the walk. She says, now go on.

DEAR FRIENDS

Whales are moving along the coast
again, headed north after tropical
months birthing, feeding, strengthening
for the return home. Now young males appear
as sentinels, and soon mothers
languidly tending their young will linger
a while, spouting, rolling in spring's muddy
ocean, signaling another turn
of the wheel.

I tarry along the shore
remembering how whales swim underneath
an ailing mate to help her rise to reach
the surface and the life of air, then guide
her safely down again and on and on
until she heals or floats away upon
the ebbing tide.

In this tough year of loss
I think of all the friends who fed me,
loved me, warmed my house and heart, trusting
the circle to hold. I want you to know
like whales, just so, you held me up as I
was letting go.

TRY NOT TO WORRY

Other people get to have stomach aches,
a day or two where they're down with the flu
or a bad headache. *For goodness sakes,*
it happens to everyone, including you,
I'm told when I worry. But I know
that innocent time is gone forever.
For me and those like me, an ache is no
simple thing. A back pain is never
just something to rub with tiger balm.
RED ALERT!! SHE HAS A PAIN. CANCER
MIGHT BE BACK AGAIN. So hard to stay calm
with that disquieting voice and no answer.
Memories of what happened back then
keep me watching for what could happen again.

BATTLE SCAR

The coffee-colored line meanders
from its hidden beginnings below,
widens in little puffs, then wanders
alongside the poor button and flows
upward, ending abruptly between breasts.
Unnatural, it runs from valley
to mountains, the scalpel's biting jest,
zipper bottom to top. There are many
in this tribe, this secret sorority
of bisected bellies and raw red lines.
We travel toward eternity,
cancer comrades on cosmic time.

RELIC

The half-buried sundial rests in weeds
and tall grasses on its side, whispering
its bitter reminder all the same: Grow old
along with me. The best is yet to be.

An assured statement, simple, confident.
And so we were two years ago. Our lives
unfolded before us, singular
map to tomorrow, there for the reading.

Now we inhabit a different star. Now
there is today and we are grateful
for it. Blessed be a painless morning.
We wake together. We touch. We love.

This is the sun we stand in today.
This is why we threw the sundial away.

MY ANGEL COMES TO ME IN DREAMS

My angel comes to me in dreams
speaking lilting luminous lines that say
significant things about death. It seems
I am in a crowded mall, watching a play

where an angel speaks about dying.
I am touched but untouched. A shopping mall
presents angelic show business, no crying
allowed. When he retreats over a hill

through a golden grove blazing with light,
I stand, silent and soul-stricken,
watching him go down in glory. My flight
is on hold while Ohio's fog thickens.

Managing cancer, I live tucked between
shopping and angels, with bittersweet dreams.

HOW MUCH TIME DO I HAVE?

The doctor says two years
from when the tumor comes back.
My friends' eyes say soon
or never.
I say, today
I feel ok.
But when I work in the garden
and bend long to the tasks
of weeding and planting,
then straighten and stretch
in late afternoon sun
among lilies and lilacs
two ospreys circling
above, oh, then
surprised and grateful
for another spring
and this body still standing
I wonder how I could leave
such beauty, such joy
and I bow low in the garden again.

A LOVE POEM

Old packhorse body, you carry me
as best you can through every kind of day.
From rotund belly to scarred right knee
you're as familiar to me as the way
home, say, or an egg or this morning's rain.
You stoop, turn and carry as needed.
Few twinges. Your strength's back again.
You move nourishment through me unheeded
and take what you need while I rest.
I love your long bones and intricate levers,
your strong hands, freckled skin, bouncing breasts,
your smells and your sounds and your savors.
I love you more now that I know,
sooner than I want to, I must let you go.

river runs
its own way
its own why
let it flow
row

A photograph of a tunnel in the side of a mountain is tacked up in front of my desk to remind me about fear. I took it the summer we rented a small recreational vehicle and traveled to Zion National Park in Southern Utah. At the lower entrance to the park, a sign reminds visitors of an exit tunnel on the other side, telling RV drivers to BE CAREFUL—the tunnel is xxx feet high. We drove on and spent a golden autumn day in Zion, climbing to emerald pools and wading clear cold streams at the end of the canyon. With me all day was an image: the RV, stuck like a cork in a bottle in the long dark tunnel.

Of course, when we finally left the park and drove through this "long dark tunnel," our vehicle breezed out and into the light. Later, trying to recall that glorious day in Zion, I realized I had never really been there. I lived that day in fear of what might happen . . . and it never did.

So here is cancer. There is a tunnel in my future, perhaps soon, perhaps not so soon, but a tunnel for certain. I look at the photograph and remind myself to stay awake now. In the twilight, an oriole calls. The dog raises his head, ears squared, alert for foraging deer. A light is on in Marty's studio and music drifts through the open door. Today is a good day. And one way or another, I'm going back to Zion.

SAY YES QUICKLY

Get over it. There's a tear in the fabric
of forever and it's just the way
it is. God didn't tap you on the back
because you were a bad girl and today
you pay for it. You did nothing wrong.
It wasn't all the walks you didn't take
or Irish luck that tossed you headlong
into cancer. Consider this a wake-
up call and live your gift of days with joy.
Walk the edge where air is thin and clear,
where fear can take you further. It's just
another country. Chin up. Step through the door.

Each breath in a miracle.
Each breath out a letting go.

CHACO CANYON

a long time coming
and a long road in
ravens circle
ruined kivas
still here
after all these years
witness
this basin of ghosts
and swooping swallows
this brown boulder
sliced clean off
the mountain
this silence
this full chorus
of time

SAILING BACK TO SHIPROCK

In this country nothing
is easy.
Rolling across high canyons
dusty brown speckled with sage,
noon sun beats against
car windows, melts
the unfurling road.
There is little shelter
except ragged Gas Man stations
hours apart and stale
ice cream in chattering freezers.
We come from the red hills of Zion
and Chaco's sandy ruined stones.
At night the coyote called
to us across dreams, across time.
Now we look for fast food
to fuel our fast trip
I was going to say home
but I think that
is what we left behind.
Look,
we are climbing back down
into the hole in the center
of the earth, we are turned
toward the west, we are
determined to leave,
we are sailing back to Shiprock
steadied under a wide sky,
salt on our lips
salt in our eyes.

PAH TEMPE

Circle come round
to the Virgin River,
canyon hot springs,
Paiute healing waters.
Sulfur smells, rising bubbles
erase a dozen years
in a fluid moment
of dry breeze in cottonwoods
flashing along the stone path.
Today there is a woman
close to death
in the river,
a sack of guts
and languid long bones
and lighted eyes
bobbing inside a plastic innertube.
Two young women hold her upright.
Small boys splash around her,
shouting "watch me! watch me!"
Later, when the sun is lower,
strong arms will lift her out
of the river and carry her
back along the whispering path.
But now
in this blessed moment
we are in the water together
floating, floating
in this sacred place
this blood-red canyon
where hawks fly overhead
and sooner or later
we will all soar.

GETTING STRONGER EVERY DAY

Morning

A thousand years ago
someone's hands arranged these rocks
into walls. I bend
in the doorway, enter
a small dark room—
so this is how it was,
wet earthen smells rising
from the ground, voices
distant and indistinct.
People were busy here,
cool in the noon sun,
warm in the cooling evening.
Outside in the rubbish heaps
tiny painted shards
remember water jugs
and the hands that shaped
the coils.
We struggle to reassemble,
to find the reasoned
structure
in the stones.

Twilight

In the arroyo the ruins stand
simply against a rain-filled sky.
Low walls meet at the join,
rising gradually upward.
A raven is walking among the rubble.
I am here at the kiva,

witness to the fallen stones.
Deep in the canyon
we live the beauty of the chaos
until darkness
is complete.

Two A.M.

Coyote yips and howls
from within sandstone shadows.
I am called from my dreams
to a restless campground
and in a flash I understand
how to hold this cancer
I have taken on the road:
not rummaging in rubbish heaps
for shards of meaning
or walking among the ruins
of yesterday's structures,
but holding this moment
against time's broader horizon
and breathing
a grateful blessing.
Outside there is no moon
and no water.
Still, the Trickster sings.
Still, my wild heart beats.

A NOTE ABOUT THE AUTHOR

Mary Bradish O'Connor was born in 1942 in Appleton, Wisconsin, the hometown of Joe McCarthy and Harry Houdini. She has graduate degrees from the University of Wisconsin–Madison and John F. Kennedy University. Like a whale accumulates barnacles, she has accumulated life experiences as a psychotherapist, editor, Latin teacher, professional grooming instructor, dean of students, wife, person with cancer, lesbian, Catholic and Buddhist, country woman and book critic. This is her second book of poetry.

COLOPHON

This book was typeset in Goudy, a typeface designed by American typographer Frederic Goudy early in the 20th century. It was chosen for its legibility and classic appearance, and in honor of the designer's mentor, Stephanie Kroninger, who died of breast cancer in 1993.

The book is printed on Champion Mystique Text, an acid-free, 50% recycled paper (20% post-consumer recovered fiber), and manufactured by Data Reproductions Inc., Michigan.